80
AND
PROUD
OF IT

summersdale

80 AND PROUD OF IT

Copyright © Summersdale Publishers Ltd, 2014

With text contributed by Yvette Jane

All rights reserved.

No part of this book may be reproduced by any means, nor transmitted, nor translated into a machine language, without the written permission of the publishers.

Condition of Sale
This book is sold subject to the condition that it shall not, by way of trade or otherwise, be lent, re-sold, hired out or otherwise circulated in any form of binding or cover other than that in which it is published and without a similar condition including this condition being imposed on the subsequent purchaser.

Summersdale Publishers Ltd
46 West Street
Chichester
West Sussex
PO19 1RP
UK

www.summersdale.com

Printed and bound in the Czech Republic

ISBN: 978-1-84953-566-3

Substantial discounts on bulk quantities of Summersdale books are available to corporations, professional associations and other organisations. For details contact Nicky Douglas by telephone: +44 (0) 1243 756902, fax: +44 (0) 1243 786300 or email: nicky@summersdale.com.

TO...

FROM...

CONTENTS

ANOTHER
YEAR
OLDER

GETTING OLDER IS NO
PROBLEM. YOU JUST
HAVE TO LIVE LONG
ENOUGH.

Groucho Marx

IF THINGS GET BETTER
WITH AGE THEN YOU
ARE APPROACHING
MAGNIFICENT.

Anonymous

AT THE AGE OF
80, EVERYTHING
REMINDS YOU OF
SOMETHING ELSE.

Lowell Thomas

BY THE TIME YOU'RE
80 YEARS OLD YOU'VE
LEARNED EVERYTHING.
YOU ONLY HAVE TO
REMEMBER IT.

George Burns

AGE IS SOMETHING THAT DOESN'T MATTER, UNLESS YOU ARE A CHEESE.

Billie Burke

YOU'RE WRITING THE STORY OF YOUR LIFE ONE MOMENT AT A TIME.

Doc Childre and Howard Martin

YOU ARE NEVER TOO
OLD TO SET ANOTHER
GOAL OR TO DREAM
A NEW DREAM.

C. S. Lewis

WE ARE ALWAYS THE SAME AGE INSIDE.

Gertrude Stein

THE OLDER THE FIDDLE, THE SWEETER THE TUNE.

English proverb

A MAN OF 80 HAS OUTLIVED PROBABLY THREE NEW SCHOOLS OF PAINTING, TWO OF ARCHITECTURE AND POETRY AND A HUNDRED IN DRESS.

Lord Byron

LIFE IS A JOURNEY AND
WHERE YOUR FINISH
LINE IS HAS YET TO BE
DETERMINED.

Anonymous

MY SEVENTIES WERE
INTERESTING AND
FAIRLY SERENE, BUT
MY EIGHTIES ARE
PASSIONATE. I GROW
MORE INTENSE
AS I AGE.

Florida Scott-Maxwell

OUR BIRTHDAYS ARE FEATHERS IN THE BROAD WING OF TIME.

Jean Paul

YOU CAN'T TURN BACK THE CLOCK, BUT YOU CAN WIND IT UP AGAIN.

Bonnie Prudden

THE ADVANTAGE OF
BEING 80 YEARS OLD
IS THAT ONE HAS MANY
PEOPLE TO LOVE.

Jean Renoir

THE GREAT THING ABOUT
GETTING OLDER IS THAT
YOU DON'T LOSE ALL
THE OTHER AGES
YOU'VE BEEN.

Madeleine L'Engle

DON'T FIGHT THE RIVER, IT FLOWS ON ITS OWN.

Anonymous

JUST

WHAT

I ALWAYS

WANTED

THERE ARE 364 DAYS
WHEN YOU MIGHT
GET UN-BIRTHDAY
PRESENTS... AND ONLY
ONE FOR BIRTHDAY
PRESENTS, YOU KNOW.

Lewis Carroll

GOD GAVE US THE GIFT
OF LIFE; IT IS UP TO US
TO GIVE OURSELVES THE
GIFT OF LIVING WELL.

Voltaire

IT IS LOVELY, WHEN I
FORGET ALL BIRTHDAYS,
INCLUDING MY OWN, TO
FIND THAT SOMEBODY
REMEMBERS ME.

Ellen Glasgow

LET US CELEBRATE THE OCCASION WITH WINE AND SWEET WORDS.

Plautus

A COMFORTABLE OLD AGE IS THE REWARD OF A WELL-SPENT YOUTH.

Maurice Chevalier

FOR YEARS I WANTED
TO BE OLDER, AND
NOW I AM.

Margaret Atwood

THE BEST THINGS IN LIFE AREN'T THINGS.

Art Buchwald

YOUR BIRTHDAY IS A SPECIAL TIME TO CELEBRATE THE GIFT OF YOU TO THE WORLD.

Anonymous

ONE OF THE SECRETS
OF A HAPPY LIFE IS
CONTINUOUS SMALL
TREATS.

Iris Murdoch

YOUTH IS THE GIFT OF
NATURE, BUT AGE IS A
WORK OF ART.

Garson Kanin

A HUG IS THE PERFECT
GIFT; ONE SIZE FITS ALL,
AND NOBODY MINDS IF
YOU EXCHANGE IT.

Anonymous

FOR CERTAINLY OLD AGE HAS A GREAT SENSE OF CALM AND FREEDOM.

Plato

I DIDN'T GET OLD ON
PURPOSE, IT JUST
HAPPENED. IF YOU'RE
LUCKY, IT COULD
HAPPEN TO YOU.

Andy Rooney

IF INSTEAD OF A GEM,
OR EVEN A FLOWER, WE
SHOULD CAST THE GIFT
OF A LOVING THOUGHT
INTO THE HEART OF A
FRIEND, THAT WOULD
BE GIVING AS THE
ANGELS GIVE.

George MacDonald

GRIN
AND
BEAR
IT

NO WISE MAN EVER WISHED TO BE YOUNGER.

Jonathan Swift

I STILL HAVE A FULL
DECK; I JUST SHUFFLE
SLOWER NOW.

Anonymous

OLD AGE IS THE MOST
UNEXPECTED OF ALL
THE THINGS THAT CAN
HAPPEN TO A MAN.

Leon Trotsky

YOU CAN'T HELP
GETTING OLDER, BUT
YOU DON'T HAVE TO
GET OLD.

George Burns

NOT A SHRED OF
EVIDENCE EXISTS IN
FAVOUR OF THE IDEA
THAT LIFE IS SERIOUS.

Brendan Gill

NO ONE IS SO OLD AS TO THINK HE CANNOT LIVE ONE MORE YEAR.

Cicero

AGEING IS NOT 'LOST YOUTH' BUT A NEW STAGE OF OPPORTUNITY AND STRENGTH.

Betty Friedan

TOO OLD TO PLANT
TREES FOR MY OWN
GRATIFICATION, I SHALL
DO IT FOR MY POSTERITY.

Thomas Jefferson

EVERYONE IS A BORE
TO SOMEONE. THAT IS
UNIMPORTANT. THE
THING TO AVOID IS BEING
A BORE TO ONESELF.

Gerald Brenan

THE OLDER I GET, THE LESS I SUFFER FOOLS GLADLY.

Kathleen Turner

YOU KNOW YOU'RE
GETTING OLDER WHEN
YOU NOTICE MORE
AND MORE HISTORY
QUESTIONS HAPPENED IN
YOUR LIFETIME.

Tom Wilson

OUR TODAYS DEPEND ON
OUR YESTERDAYS AND
OUR TOMORROWS DEPEND
ON OUR TODAYS.

Elisabeth Kübler-Ross

GETTING OLD
IS A BIT LIKE
GETTING DRUNK;
EVERYONE
ELSE LOOKS
BRILLIANT.

Billy Connolly

MEMORY IS THE PLACE
WHERE OUR VANISHED
DAYS SECRETLY
GATHER, PROVIDING A
BEAUTIFUL SHELTER
AND CONTINUITY OF
IDENTITY.

John O'Donohue

IT IS AN ILLUSION
THAT YOUTH IS HAPPY,
AN ILLUSION OF THOSE
WHO HAVE LOST IT.

W. Somerset Maugham

REGRETS AND
RECRIMINATIONS ONLY
HURT YOUR SOUL.

Armand Hammer

THE OLDER YOU GET THE STRONGER THE WIND GETS AND IT'S ALWAYS IN YOUR FACE.

Jack Nicklaus

DO A LITTLE DANCE, MAKE A LITTLE LOVE

HE WHO LAUGHS, LASTS!

Mary Pettibone Poole

ONE OF THE BEST PARTS
OF BECOMING OLDER?
YOU CAN FLIRT ALL
YOU LIKE SINCE YOU'VE
BECOME HARMLESS.

Liz Smith

LOVE DOESN'T MAKE THE
WORLD GO ROUND. LOVE
IS WHAT MAKES THE
RIDE WORTHWHILE.

Franklin P. Jones

EVERY NOW AND THEN, BITE OFF MORE THAN YOU CAN CHEW.

Kobi Yamada

YOU CAN ONLY PERCEIVE REAL BEAUTY IN A PERSON AS THEY GET OLDER.

Anouk Aimée

LIFE NEEDS TO BE
APPRECIATED MORE
THAN IT NEEDS TO BE
UNDERSTOOD.

Stuart Heller

I CELEBRATE MYSELF, AND SING MYSELF.

Walt Whitman

IT'S IMPORTANT TO
HAVE A TWINKLE IN
YOUR WRINKLE.

Anonymous

MY ADVICE FOR LIFE:
DANCE AND SING YOUR
SONG WHILE THE PARTY
IS STILL ON.

Rasheed Ogunlaru

THE AGEING PROCESS
HAS YOU FIRMLY IN ITS
GRASP IF YOU NEVER
GET THE URGE TO
THROW A SNOWBALL.

Doug Larson

THE QUESTION IS NOT
WHETHER WE WILL DIE,
BUT HOW WE WILL LIVE.

Joan Borysenko

SMILE, IT'S FREE THERAPY.

Doug Horton

QUIT HANGING ON TO
THE HANDRAILS... LET
GO. SURRENDER. GO FOR
THE RIDE OF YOUR LIFE.
DO IT EVERY DAY.

Melody Beattie

GROW OLD ALONG
WITH ME!
THE BEST IS YET
TO BE.

Robert Browning

IF YOU OBEY ALL THE RULES, YOU MISS ALL THE FUN.

Katharine Hepburn

LIFE IS EITHER A
DARING ADVENTURE
OR NOTHING.

Helen Keller

OLD AGE IS AN
EXCELLENT TIME FOR
OUTRAGE. MY GOAL IS
TO SAY OR DO AT LEAST
ONE OUTRAGEOUS THING
EVERY WEEK.

Louis Kronenberger

IT'S NEVER TOO LATE –
IN FICTION OR IN
LIFE – TO REVISE.

Nancy Thayer

LAUGHTER DOESN'T REQUIRE TEETH.

Bill Newton

YOUNG
AT
HEART

THE HEART THAT LOVES
IS ALWAYS YOUNG.

Greek proverb

HOW OLD WOULD YOU BE IF YOU DIDN'T KNOW HOW OLD YOU WERE?

Satchel Paige

IF YOU CARRY YOUR CHILDHOOD WITH YOU, YOU NEVER BECOME OLDER.

Tom Stoppard

AGE DOES NOT
DIMINISH THE EXTREME
DISAPPOINTMENT OF
HAVING A SCOOP OF
ICE CREAM FALL
FROM THE CONE.

Jim Fiebig

IF I KEEP A GREEN
BOUGH IN MY HEART,
THEN THE SINGING BIRD
WILL COME.

Chinese proverb

LOVE HAS MORE DEPTH
AS YOU GET OLDER.

Kirk Douglas

THE GARDENER'S RULE
APPLIES TO YOUTH AND
AGE: WHEN YOUNG, SOW
WILD OATS, BUT WHEN
OLD, GROW SAGE.

H. J. Byron

I WANT TO DIE YOUNG AT A RIPE OLD AGE.

Ashley Montagu

YEARS MAY WRINKLE
THE SKIN, BUT TO
GIVE UP ENTHUSIASM
WRINKLES THE SOUL.

Samuel Ullman

WHEN I WAS YOUNGER,
I COULD REMEMBER
ANYTHING, WHETHER IT
HAPPENED OR NOT.

Mark Twain

JUST REMEMBER,
ONCE YOU'RE OVER THE
HILL YOU BEGIN TO
PICK UP SPEED.

Charles M. Schulz

IN OUR DREAMS WE ARE
ALWAYS YOUNG.

Sarah Louise Delany

SOME DAY YOU WILL
BE OLD ENOUGH TO
START READING FAIRY
TALES AGAIN.

C. S. Lewis

YOU ARE ONLY YOUNG
ONCE, BUT YOU CAN BE
IMMATURE FOR
A LIFETIME.

John P. Grier

THERE IS NO OLD AGE.
THERE IS, AS THERE
ALWAYS WAS, JUST YOU.

Carol Matthau

WE TURN NOT OLDER WITH YEARS, BUT NEWER EVERY DAY.

Emily Dickinson

EVERYONE IS THE AGE
OF THEIR HEART.

Guatemalan proverb

I'M HAPPY TO REPORT THAT MY INNER CHILD IS STILL AGELESS.

James Broughton

OLDER
AND
WISER?

IT'S WHAT YOU LEARN
AFTER YOU KNOW IT ALL
THAT COUNTS.

John Wooden

WISDOM DOESN'T
AUTOMATICALLY
COME WITH OLD AGE.
NOTHING DOES — EXCEPT
WRINKLES.

Abigail Van Buren

IF YOU CAN SPEND A
PERFECTLY USELESS
AFTERNOON IN A
PERFECTLY USELESS
MANNER, YOU HAVE
LEARNED HOW TO LIVE.

Lin Yutang

AGE IS A HIGH PRICE TO PAY FOR MATURITY.

Tom Stoppard

WE ARE NOT LIMITED BY OUR OLD AGE; WE ARE LIBERATED BY IT.

Stu Mittleman

IT'S NEVER TOO LATE
TO BECOME THE PERSON
YOU HAVE ALWAYS BEEN.

John Kimbrough

THE MORE SAND HAS
ESCAPED FROM THE
HOURGLASS OF OUR
LIFE, THE CLEARER
WE SHOULD SEE
THROUGH IT.

Jean Paul

WHEN THE DAY ENDS AND
THE SUN SETS, I LET MY
TROUBLES GO.

Albert Schweitzer

NEVER MISTAKE
KNOWLEDGE FOR
WISDOM. ONE HELPS YOU
MAKE A LIVING, THE
OTHER HELPS YOU
MAKE A LIFE.

Sandra Carey

WISDOM IS THE REWARD
FOR A LIFETIME OF
LISTENING WHEN
YOU'D HAVE PREFERRED
TO TALK.

Doug Larson

WE ASK FOR LONG LIFE,
BUT 'TIS DEEP LIFE,
OR NOBLE MOMENTS
THAT SIGNIFY. LET
THE MEASURE OF TIME
BE SPIRITUAL, NOT
MECHANICAL.

Ralph Waldo Emerson

EDUCATION IS THE BEST
PROVISION FOR THE
JOURNEY TO OLD AGE.

Aristotle

EXPERIENCE IS SIMPLY
THE NAME WE GIVE
OUR MISTAKES.

Oscar Wilde

LIFE IS SHORT AND
MESSY. DON'T POSTPONE
LIVING UNTIL LIFE GETS
NEATER OR EASIER OR
LESS FRANTIC OR MORE
ENLIGHTENED.

Oriah Mountain Dreamer

I SPEAK THE TRUTH NOT
SO MUCH AS I WOULD,
BUT AS MUCH AS I DARE,
AND I DARE A LITTLE
MORE AS I GROW OLDER.

Michel de Montaigne

THIS ABOVE ALL: TO THINE OWN SELF BE TRUE.

William Shakespeare

AS YOU GROW OLDER,
YOU LEARN TO
UNDERSTAND LIFE A
LITTLE BETTER.

Solomon Burke

LIFE CAN ONLY BE
UNDERSTOOD BACKWARDS,
BUT IT MUST BE
LIVED FORWARDS.

Søren Kierkegaard

TIME CHANGES
EVERYTHING EXCEPT
SOMETHING WITHIN
US WHICH IS ALWAYS
SURPRISED BY CHANGE.

Thomas Hardy

WISDOM DOESN'T
NECESSARILY COME
WITH AGE. SOMETIMES
AGE JUST SHOWS UP
ALL BY ITSELF.

Tom Wilson

LIVE, LOVE AND LAST

THIS IS THE ART OF THE
SOUL: TO HARVEST YOUR
DEEPER LIFE FROM ALL
THE SEASONS OF YOUR
EXPERIENCE.

John O'Donohue

MEN DO NOT QUIT
PLAYING BECAUSE THEY
GROW OLD; THEY GROW
OLD BECAUSE THEY
QUIT PLAYING.

Oliver Wendell Holmes Jr

FORGET PAST MISTAKES.
FORGET FAILURES.
FORGET EVERYTHING
EXCEPT WHAT YOU ARE
GOING TO DO NOW
AND DO IT.

Will Durant

I LOVE EVERYTHING
THAT'S OLD:
OLD FRIENDS,
OLD TIMES,
OLD MANNERS,
OLD BOOKS,
OLD WINES.

Oliver Goldsmith

YOU ONLY LIVE ONCE, BUT IF YOU DO IT RIGHT, ONCE IS ENOUGH.

Mae West

AGE DOES NOT PROTECT
YOU FROM LOVE, BUT
LOVE TO SOME EXTENT
PROTECTS YOU
FROM AGE.

Jeanne Moreau

EXECUTE EVERY ACT OF
THY LIFE AS THOUGH IT
WERE THY LAST.

Marcus Aurelius

LIFE IS TOO SHORT, SO
KISS SLOWLY, LAUGH
INSANELY, LOVE TRULY
AND FORGIVE QUICKLY.

Anonymous

THE IMPORTANT THING
IS NOT HOW MANY YEARS
IN YOUR LIFE, BUT HOW
MUCH LIFE IN
YOUR YEARS!

Edward Stieglitz

THE LONGER I LIVE
THE MORE BEAUTIFUL
LIFE BECOMES.

Frank Lloyd Wright

HERE, WITH WHITENED
HAIR... HE DRANK TO
LIFE, TO ALL IT HAD
BEEN, TO WHAT IT WAS,
TO WHAT IT WOULD BE.

Sean O'Casey

I'M TOO OLD TO DO THINGS BY HALF.

Lou Reed

IF YOU ASSOCIATE
ENOUGH WITH OLDER
PEOPLE WHO ENJOY
THEIR LIVES, YOU WILL
GAIN THE POSSIBILITY
FOR A FULL LIFE.

Margaret Mead

PEOPLE ARE ALWAYS
ASKING ABOUT THE GOOD
OLD DAYS. I SAY, WHY
DON'T YOU SAY THE
GOOD NOW DAYS?

Robert M. Young

LIFE IS JUST ONE
GRAND, SWEET SONG, SO
START THE MUSIC.

Ronald Reagan

SO MAYST THOU LIVE,
DEAR! MANY YEARS,
IN ALL THE BLISS THAT
LIFE ENDEARS.

Thomas Hood

ILLS,
PILLS
AND
TWINGES

OLDER PEOPLE
SHOULDN'T EAT HEALTH
FOOD, THEY NEED ALL
THE PRESERVATIVES
THEY CAN GET.

Robert Orben

AS YOU GET OLDER
THREE THINGS HAPPEN.
THE FIRST IS YOUR
MEMORY GOES, AND I
CAN'T REMEMBER THE
OTHER TWO...

– Norman Wisdom

IF WRINKLES MUST BE
WRITTEN UPON OUR
BROWS, LET THEM NOT
BE WRITTEN UPON THE
HEART. THE SPIRIT
SHOULD NEVER
GROW OLD.

James A. Garfield

WHEN YOU LIVE IN THE MOMENT, EVEN YOUR 'SENIOR MOMENTS' DON'T MATTER.

Dr Bernie S. Siegel

AS YOU GET OLDER, THE
PICKINGS GET SLIMMER,
BUT THE PEOPLE DON'T.

Carrie Fisher

MY DOCTOR TOLD ME
TO DO SOMETHING
THAT PUTS ME OUT OF
BREATH, SO I'VE TAKEN
UP SMOKING AGAIN.

Jo Brand

OLD PEOPLE ARE FOND
OF GIVING GOOD ADVICE;
IT CONSOLES THEM
FOR NO LONGER BEING
CAPABLE OF SETTING A
BAD EXAMPLE.

François de La Rochefoucauld

YOU KNOW YOU'RE OLD IF THEY HAVE DISCONTINUED YOUR BLOOD TYPE.

Phyllis Diller

GRANT ME CHASTITY AND CONTINENCE, BUT NOT YET.

Augustine of Hippo

MEN GROW OLD, PEARLS
GROW YELLOW; THERE IS
NO CURE FOR IT.

Chinese proverb

AS THE ARTERIES GROW HARD, THE HEART GROWS SOFT.

H. L. Mencken

DON'T LET AGEING GET
YOU DOWN. IT'S TOO
HARD TO GET BACK UP.

John Wagner

THE SPIRITUAL
EYESIGHT IMPROVES
AS THE PHYSICAL
EYESIGHT DECLINES.

Plato

IF YOU REST,
YOU RUST.

Helen Hayes

CHIN UP, CHEST OUT

IF YOU SURVIVE LONG
ENOUGH, YOU'RE
REVERED – RATHER LIKE
AN OLD BUILDING.

Katharine Hepburn

BECAUSE OF YOUR SMILE,
YOU MAKE LIFE MORE
BEAUTIFUL.

Thích Nhất Hạnh

LET US RESPECT GREY HAIRS, ESPECIALLY OUR OWN.

J. P. Sears

WHEN GRACE IS JOINED
WITH WRINKLES, IT IS
ADORABLE. THERE IS AN
UNSPEAKABLE DAWN IN
HAPPY OLD AGE.

Victor Hugo

A DIAMOND IS JUST A
PIECE OF CHARCOAL
THAT HANDLED STRESS
EXCEPTIONALLY WELL.

Anonymous

THE OLDER I GET THE MORE OF MY MOTHER I SEE IN MYSELF.

Nancy Friday

DON'T RETOUCH MY
WRINKLES... I WOULD
NOT WANT IT TO BE
THOUGHT THAT I
HAD LIVED FOR ALL
THESE YEARS WITHOUT
SOMETHING TO SHOW
FOR IT.

Queen Elizabeth, The Queen Mother

TO BEGIN ANEW, WE
MUST SAY GOODBYE TO
WHO WE ONCE WERE.

Anonymous

I'M LIKE A GOOD CHEESE.
I'M JUST GETTING
MOULDY ENOUGH TO BE
INTERESTING.

Paul Newman

EVERY WRINKLE IS BUT A NOTCH IN THE QUIET CALENDAR OF A WELL-SPENT LIFE.

Charles Dickens

@EsmeTheBird

If you're interested in finding out more about our books, find us on Facebook at **Summersdale Publishers** and follow us on Twitter at **@Summersdale**.

www.summersdale.com